Steve

To remind you of us + where we live.
Hope you had a wonderful birthday.

Much love

Wayne, Tania, Erin, Joshua + Rhys

2005

x x x x x

The Shoalhaven
SOUTH COAST NEW SOUTH WALES
Revisited

Photography by
SUE and BRIAN KENDRICK

A Lightstorm Publication

Published by Lightstorm Publishing ©
Distributed by Lightstorm Photography
P.O. Box 1167 Nowra NSW 2541
Ph: (02) 4446 0911 Fax: (02) 4446 0922
Email: lightsto@ozemail.com.au

First published December 2002
© Copyright: photographs and text
Sue and Brian Kendrick 2002
Printed by PMP Print, Australia

National Library of Australia
Cataloguing-in-Publication data
Shoalhaven, The: South Coast New South Wales
Kendrick, Sue; Kendrick, Brian(ill)

ISBN 0-9586745-3-1.

All rights reserved. Subject to the Copyright Act 1968, no part of this publication may be reproduced, stored in a retrieval system, or transmitted in any form, by any means, electronic, mechanical, photocopying, recording, or otherwise, without the prior written permission of the publisher.

Title Page: Old Mans Hat, Beecroft Peninsula.
Right: An aerial view of Culburra showing Greenwell Point, Comerong Island and Coolangatta Mountain in the distance.
Below: A male Superb Lyrebird displaying its striking tail feathers. The lyrebird is the faunal emblem of the Shoalhaven.   Photo courtesy Rob Watkins.

CONTENTS

Introduction	7
History	10
Towns and Villages	19
Parks and Reserves	51
Arthur Boyd's Bundanon	59
The Royal Australian Navy	63
Industries	67
University	71
Lightstorm Photo Gallery	72

INTRODUCTION

The Shoalhaven district is located on the New South Wales coast, 160 kilometres south of Sydney. Stretching from the picturesque town of Berry in the north to Durras in the south, its eastern border is fringed by pristine beaches of white sand interspersed with dramatic sandstone cliffs and rocky headlands, while the mountains of the Morton and Budawang National Parks stand sentinel over its western extremity.

The original inhabitants of the region were Aborigines from the Wodi Wodi, Dharumba and Wandandian tribes, who have lived in the Shoalhaven region for more than 20,000 years. The first European to sight the area was Captain Cook, who named Pigeon House Mountain in April 1770, but it wasn't until 1797 that George Bass gave the area its name. He discovered the mouth of a river, well guarded by shoals, which he named `Shoals Haven´. Although he was actually describing the mouth of the Crookhaven River the name was subsequently applied to the main river and later to the district. Apart from itinerant settlement by cedar cutters and whalers the area remained largely uninhabited by Europeans until Alexander Berry and Edward Wollstonecraft took up a lease of 10,000 acres on the northern bank of the Shoalhaven River in 1822. These days, the Shoalhaven region is home to more than 85,000 people and is one of the fastest growing localities in New South Wales.

An area of enormous geographic diversity, the district offers visitors an opportunity to experience a wide range of activities. Anglers, surfers, sailboard riders and swimmers have over 100 beaches to choose from, including Hyams Beach, which boasts the whitest sand in the world. Rock climbers come from near and far to tackle the near vertical cliffs of Point Perpendicular, while scuba divers enjoy the clear water and unique marine life of Jervis Bay. Yachting enthusiasts revel in the region's spectacular sailing while bushwalkers and canoeists find their challenge in the mountains and rivers of Morton and Budawang National Parks. The region's natural treasures are protected in over 300,000 hectares of Parks and Reserves.

The towns of the Shoalhaven offer a variety of temptations. Berry, town of trees, is famous for its antique and specialty shops, while Kangaroo Valley boasts numerous beautiful craft shops. Nowra, with a population of more than 25,000 is the administrative and commercial centre of the region and provides all services. The delightful village of Huskisson is the stepping off point for scuba diving, penguin, dolphin, whale and seal watching tours, while further south the fishing port of Ulladulla and its neighbouring town Mollymook, is a popular centre for golf, surfing, fishing and diving. Between these points are several small towns and villages, each offering their own special appeal.

Dairy farming and forest industries have been important to the region since the early days of European settlement, and in more recent times manufacturing and processing industries such as the Manildra Group, Shoalhaven Paper and Dairy Farmers Co-operative have become important to the regional economy.

The Royal Australian Navy has had a presence in the district since 1915 when the R.A.N. College was constructed at Jervis Bay. During the Second World War the British navy established a Fleet Air Arm base near Nowra Hill, which was transferred to the R.A.N. in 1948 and commissioned as HMAS Albatross.

In the same year the councils of Nowra, Numbaa, Shoalhaven, Broughton Vale, Broughton Creek, Bomaderry, Ulladulla, Berry, Cambewarra and Clyde amalgamated to form the Shire of Shoalhaven. Today, tourism is the major industry in a region whose scenic beauty attracts more than two million visitors each year.

Right: The near vertical cliffs of Point Perpendicular form the northern entrance to Jervis Bay.

Below: Point Perpendicular Lighthouse was built from Conjola sandstone in 1899 after years of complaint from sailors regarding the Cape St George Lighthouse a few kilometres to the south. Constructed in 1860, the Cape St George Lighthouse had apparently been built in the wrong location and could not be seen by ships approaching from the south! After construction of the new light at Point Perpendicular, the Cape St George light became a navigational hazard during daylight hours so was used by the navy as a target for bombing practise from the sea and is now a crumbling ruin. An automatic solar-powered light replaced the original Point Perpendicular light in 1993.

HISTORY

ABORIGINAL HISTORY

Twenty thousand years ago, the most recent ice age was coming to an end and the Shoalhaven coastline was approximately 20 kilometres further east than it is today. At that time, the region was already inhabited by Aborigines, but as the ice melted the sea level rose slowly, burying much of the archaeological evidence of habitation beneath metres of sea and sand. The sea reached its present level approximately 6,000 years ago and from this time numerous archaeological sites survive, which provide evidence of the Aboriginal lifestyle. Excavation has revealed the shells of edible shellfish, bones of fish, the remains of a variety of mammals, charcoal, hearthstones, bone and shell artifacts.

Seafood formed the basis of the Aboriginal diet and shell middens provide evidence of the types of food which were eaten. Until 1,000 years ago shellfish were collected and fish were caught in the mouths of estuaries and close to the shore, but more recently bark canoes were used to fish further offshore. Bowen Island offered good hunting, where penguins and mutton birds were captured and bones from these animals are found both on the island and in shell middens on the mainland. Small marsupials from the forests fringing the coast formed a regular part of the diet, while larger sea mammals such as seals were also eaten occasionally. Although plant foods would undoubtedly have formed a major part of the diet, little evidence of this remains. With such a bountiful and varied supply of food and a temperate climate it is thought that the indigenous people would have enjoyed a good lifestyle.

Tools were manufactured from bone, stone or shell. Flaked stone artifacts such as cutting and scraping tools, spear barbs and points have been excavated from campsite locations throughout the Shoalhaven. Due to the soft nature of the local stone, stone for axe-heads was traded from considerable distances. Axe grinding grooves, where the heads were ground to a smooth cutting edge, can be seen on sandstone outcrops such as the stream bed above Mary Bay. Although evidence of rock art is not extensive in the region, paintings have been found in rock shelters on the Beecroft Peninsula.

Aboriginal names are prominent as place names throughout the region. Coolangatta means splendid view, Culburra means sand, Myola is a place of crabs and Nowra is the word for black cockatoo. Ulladulla is a corruption of the Aboriginal word Woolahderra which meant safe harbour and Cambewarra is a combination of two words, `cambe' meaning fire and `warra' meaning mountain, probably because of the Illawarra flame trees which used to grow there. Captain Cook bestowed the name Pigeon House Mountain on the remarkable outcrop of stone which dominates the skyline in the south of the region, but the Aboriginal people knew it as as Dithol, which means woman's breast.

The first encounter the Aborigines had with Europeans were merely two races sighting each other from a distance. It wasn't until 1797 that direct contact first occurred, when survivors from a ship wreck at Point Hicks in Victoria were making their way northward. As they travelled through the lands of many different tribes they were received in a friendly manner where it was perceived they were passing through, and with hostility if they were viewed as permanent invaders.

In the latter years of the eighteenth century the indigenous people would have witnessed regular visits from whalers and cedar cutters, but it wasn't until Alexander Berry took up a grant of 10,000 acres on the Shoalhaven River in 1822 that settlement by Europeans commenced in earnest and the traditional lifestyle of the Aboriginal people was threatened. Once the country was stocked with sheep and cattle, many of the edible plants disappeared and the Aborigines were forced away from their traditional hunting grounds. Contact with Europeans also brought new diseases such as smallpox, influenza, measles and syphilis. During the early decades of the 19th century, some traditional food gathering practices were maintained, but by the 1830's the former population had been decimated by the combined effects of disease and the removal of land and those who remained were relocated to reserves such as Roseby Park at Orient Point and Bilong at Myola.

By 1914 small groups of Aboriginal fisherman had settled at Wreck Bay, south of Jervis Bay, and in 1954 the area was gazetted as an Aboriginal Reserve. In the 1920's the community numbered less than thirty people, but today Wreck Bay is home to nearly 200 residents. The Wreck Bay Community were granted land rights over an area of 403 hectares in 1986 and in June 1995 title to the lands and waters of Jervis Bay National Park and Jervis Bay Botanic Gardens were transferred to the Wreck Bay Aboriginal Community Council, who jointly manage both areas with the National Parks and Wildlife Service.

Right: Honeymoon Bay, a protected inlet situated on the northern side of Jervis Bay, has significance for the local Aboriginal communities as a 'keeping place'.

EXPLORATION AND SETTLEMENT

The first sighting of the Shoalhaven region by Europeans probably took place as Captain Cook and his crew sailed northward along the New South Wales coast in the HMAS Endeavour during April 1770. In his log Cook described "a remarkable peaked hill which resembled a square dove house with a dome on top", which he called Pigeon House Mountain. Further north, he noted in his log the entrance to Jervis Bay, but sailed on without giving it a name. His journal reveals that he was taking advantage of favourable winds and to "beat up" would have taken more time than he was prepared to spare. Had he decided to investigate he would have discovered the deepest natural harbour in Australia.

Twenty one years later Lieutenant Bowen named the bay Port Jervis (in honour of his former naval commander Sir John Jervis), when he sailed into its protected waters in the *Atlantic* seeking shelter from adverse winds. Although Bowen and his crew did not go ashore he noted in his log "the wisdom of training young naval officers in seamanship here".

Whilst others visited the region in the ensuing years, it wasn't until 1797 that George Bass gave the region its name on his epic journey south in an open whaleboat. He discovered the mouth of a river, well guarded by sandy shoals, which he named Shoals Haven. Although he was actually describing the mouth of the Crookhaven River, the name was soon applied to the main river and eventually to the region. Bass was unimpressed with the country he saw, describing it as generally barren, although he did note that the area to the south of the bay may prove suitable for cattle.

The first European settlement was of an itinerant nature; whalers worked out of the safe haven of Jervis Bay and timber cutters felled red cedar in the forests. But it wasn't until 1811 that any serious exploration occurred when surveyor George Evans came ashore near the present town of Huskisson. He journeyed along Currambene Creek, crossed the Shoalhaven River west of Nowra then climbed Mount Cambewarra. When Surveyor General John Oxley visited the area eight years later he described what he saw as "miserable, sterile country" and noted that he could see no place where "even a cabbage might be planted with a prospect of success".

Despite such discouraging reports, Alexander Berry recognised the potential of the region for farming after exploration of the area in early

Left: Hampden Bridge, which spans the Kangaroo River in Kangaroo Valley, was completed in May 1898. The wooden suspension bridge with castellated sandstone pylons is the only bridge of its type remaining in Australia. Just five days after its completion the old bridge was washed away by floodwaters.

1822. Six months later he and his partner Edward Wollstonecraft took up a grant of 10,000 acres (4,047 hectares) on the Shoalhaven River in exchange for the maintenance of 100 convicts. Permanent settlement of the region then commenced in earnest.

Because of the shoals which made the mouth of the Shoalhaven River dangerous, Berry set the convicts to work cutting a canal across the narrow sand spit which separated it from the Crookhaven River. The canal was completed in just twelve days and it remains the route of egress to the sea for the Shoalhaven River. Berry chose to build his homestead at the base of the hill known by Aboriginals as Collungatta and soon a self-supporting village grew in its shadow. The new community was entirely dependent upon the river for transport of goods to and from the port of Sydney.

In the south of the region settlement commenced when Reverend Thomas Kendall received a grant of 1280 acres (518 hectares) just north of the present township of Milton, which he took up in 1828. He called the property Kendall Dale and ran cattle and felled cedar with ticket-of-leave men (paroled convicts). The surrounding area was soon taken up and became known as The Settlement, which the first postmaster later changed to Milton in honour of the great English poet. The early residents of Milton used the natural harbour seven kilometres further south, which they called Boat Harbour but the name was later changed to Ulladulla, thought to be a corruption of the Aboriginal word `Woollahderra´, which means safe harbour.

The mainstays of the regional economy in the early years of settlement were farming and timber cutting. Agricultural produce was varied; dairy products, tobacco, potatoes, maize and other crops were produced, principally for the Sydney market. In the early years wheat was grown but rust eventually affected the crop and the industry collapsed. When wool prices began to rise in the 1840's, a track called The Wool Road was cut across the mountains from Braidwood to Jervis Bay and wool and tallow became important exports.

By the early 1850's Terara, on the south bank of the Shoalhaven River, had become the commercial, social and cultural centre for the people south of the river. A series of disastrous floods in 1860, 1870 and 1874 completely destroyed the town and forced the relocation to Nowra, which was well sited on higher ground. Construction of a bridge over the Shoalhaven in 1881 to replace the punts and ferries confirmed Nowra's status as the new commercial centre of the district.

Following Federation in 1901, and the naming of Canberra as the national capital in 1911, Jervis Bay was selected as a port for the new capital. An area of land on the southern side of the bay along with Bowen Island and part of the bay itself, was transferred from New South Wales to the Commonwealth. Within these boundaries the newly formed Royal Australian Navy made recommendation for the creation of a Naval College, which was completed in 1915. Thus, Lieutenant Bowen's vision in 1791, of a training centre for naval officers, was realised. Ambitious residential developments were also planned for the shores of Jervis Bay in the light of the Government's decision to build the federal port there, but when a planned rail link with Canberra failed to eventuate these plans did not materialise.

Despite this, the Shoalhaven region has continued to prosper throughout the twentieth century, and today it is one of the fastest growing areas of New South Wales. The area now boasts an active manufacturing sector and recognition of the region's natural beauty means that tourism is the region's most important industry.

Left: The gymnasium building, with its striking clocktower, dominates the parade ground at HMAS Creswell, Jervis Bay. When the college took its first cadets in 1915 it fulfilled Lieutenant Bowen's prophesy of 1791 that Jervis Bay would be an ideal location for the training of young naval officers.

Below: Pigeon House Mountain, sighted by Captain Cook in April 1770, was the first landmark in the region to be given a European name. The Aboriginal people know the mountain as Dithol, which means woman's breast.

TOWNS

A large part of the Shoalhaven's appeal derives from the number of small towns and villages found within its borders. From Kangaroo Valley in the northern part of the region, with its craft and specialty shops, to the historic village of Milton in the south, the towns of the Shoalhaven offer a glimpse of the past, or an opportunity to enjoy one of the many leisure activities for which the region is famous.

Nowra

With a population of more than 25,000 Nowra is the administrative and commercial centre of the Shoalhaven region and the focus of an active manufacturing sector. In the early days of European settlement however, people were slow to settle in Nowra and the religious, cultural, social and commercial life of the district was centred around the town of Terara, located on the Shoalhaven River a few kilometres downstream.

Nowra township was declared in 1852 and some plots of land sold in 1855, but it wasn't until a disastrous flood struck Terara in 1860 that Nowra began to assume dominance as the centre of the district. Terara suffered again in the floods of 1870, thereby consolidating Nowra's growing position of importance in the region. The building of the bridge over the Shoalhaven River in 1881 adjacent to the town assured its future prosperity.

In the early years of this century the Royal Australian Navy built its training college at Jervis Bay, thereby starting a long association between the navy and the town. In 1948 HMAS Albatross was commissioned at Nowra Hill and almost half a century later the R.A.N. is the largest employer in the region.

The name Nowra derives from an aboriginal word meaning 'black cockatoo'. The black cockatoo has now become the town's emblem and features on banners, tile murals and other artwork around the town.

Cambewarra

Located at the foot of Cambewarra Mountain the name comes from two aboriginal words, 'cambe' meaning fire and 'warra' meaning mountain. Illawarra flame trees and coach wood are both common on the mountain and their reddish blooms are thought to be the inspiration for the name.

Left: The Shoalhaven River separates Nowra - on the southern side of the River - from Bomaderry and North Nowra. The original Shoalhaven River Bridge was opened to traffic in 1881; the 'new' bridge opened 99 years later.

Above right: A memorial to honour Shoalhaven Servicemen who lost their lives in WWI stands at the entrance to Nowra Showground.

Right: Cambewarra Mountain affords excellent views over the Shoalhaven from the lookout at its summit.

Berry

The northernmost town of the Shoalhaven, Berry was formerly known as Broughton Creek, possibly after an aboriginal stockman, Broughton. The name was changed in 1890 to honour the Berry family, first European settlers to the region. The land on which Berry is situated was formerly a private town on Alexander Berry's Coolangatta Estate.

The town prospered in the 1880's and many of the beautiful historic buildings which lend such character to the Berry streetscape date from this period. The Post and Telegraph Office, opened in 1886 now houses a lovely cafe; while the adjacent English Scottish and Australian Bank building houses the Berry Museum. The Commercial Bank of Sydney, built in 1889, subsequently housed the National Australia Bank but is now the Bunyip Inn guest house.

Berry is a popular weekend destination for visitors from Sydney, Canberra and Wollongong who are lured by the many wonderful antique and specialty shops, as well as the excellent choice of restaurants, bistros and cafes. A range of accommodation styles has been developed in the area to meet the growing demand and varies from luxurious self-contained houses with panoramic ocean views to quaint B&B's.

There are several excellent wineries near Berry: Bundewallah Estate, is on the outskirts of the town while Jasper Valley Winery, The Silos, Cambewarra Estate and Coolangatta Estate are just a short drive away.

On the first Sunday of each month the Berry market offers an enticing variety of local art and craft in an atmosphere of country charm.

Left: An aerial view of Berry showing its proximity to Seven Mile Beach.

Above Right: Berry is a popular shopping destination with its many galleries and specialty shops.

Right: The Berry Courthouse was built in 1891 in the classical Greek revival style. Court activities continued at Berry until 1988, after which the building was used for a time as an annexe to the Police Station. In 1994 the Courthouse was sold into private hands, but a massive local campaign saw the Courthouse returned to the community when it was purchased by Shoalhaven City Council in 1999. The Berry Courthouse Conservation Committee undertook a major restoration of the building, which is now listed on the Register of the National Trust. The gardens are a major feature of the Courthouse complex; on the eastern side a traditional hedged garden has been created while on the western side, a Xeriscape garden demonstrating water saving principles can be viewed.

The Courthouse is now used by the local community for a variety of activities including concerts, art exhibitions, weddings and other special events.

Kangaroo Valley

When explorer George Evans first set eyes on Kangaroo Valley in 1812 he saw "a view no painter could beautify". Nestled between Cambewarra and Barrengarry Mountains, Kangaroo Valley township is the centre of a rich farming district. Weathering of the volcanic Kangaroo Mountain and Broughton Head yielded lush alluvial floodplains, watered by the Kangaroo River. The valley's beauty has also attracted artists and craftsmen, and visitors are treated to a wonderful choice of local handcrafts from the many specialty shops of the valley.

The first European settlement in the valley was itinerant in nature; in 1820 Cornelius O'Brien and Captain Richard Brooks both sent cattle over the range to graze on the floodplains of the Kangaroo River and provided huts for their men in the valley. The cedar cutters followed in the 1830's and cedar cutting continued in the valley until the free selectors cleared the last remaining stands in the 1860's. The timber was sawn in pits then taken out of the valley via an inland route, much of it being used in the growing towns of Berrima and Goulburn.

In 1840 Henry Osborne was granted 2,560 acres in the centre of the valley at Barrengarry. Osborne was quick to expand his holdings and the growing settlement became known for a time as the Private Township of Osborne.

Dairy farming was soon established as the valley's principal industry and by the early 1890's there were four factories processing milk in the district.

Today, tourists are attracted by the excellent camping, hiking and canoeing opportunities, as well as the town's shops and restaurants.

Left: The fertile floodplains of the Kangaroo River are ringed by mountains.
Below: Canoeing on the Kangaroo River is a popular pastime.

Shoalhaven Heads

Located on the northern banks of the mouth of the Shoalhaven River adjacent to Seven Mile Beach, the township was originally known as Jerry Bailey. Although George Bass used the name 'Shoals Haven' to describe the mouth of the River in 1797, it wasn't until 1955 that the name officially reverted to a derivation of the original nomenclature.

People were slow to settle at 'the heads'; residents of Berry had fishing shacks there but there was little permanent occupation until the depression years, when people moved permanently to the town. These days, Shoalhaven Heads has a population approaching three thousand, which swells to more than twice that number in the summer months.

Coolangatta

Coolangatta, meaning splendid view, is the site of the first European settlement in the Shoalhaven. These days, many of the historic buildings dating from that time are preserved within the Coolangatta Estate Winery, which has been developed on the site.

Left: The township of Shoalhaven Heads is ideally located between the Shoalhaven River, Seven Mile Beach and Mount Coolangatta.

Below: Windsurfers can be seen most days riding the waves adjacent to the surf club at Shoalhaven Heads.

Greenwell Point

Located near the mouth of the Crookhaven River, fifteen kilometres east of Nowra, Greenwell Point is named after an aboriginal doctor 'Greenwell' who was famous for his treatment of toothache and snakebite.

'The Point' became the Shoalhaven's first port when Alexander Berry constructed a wharf there in 1829 to service the large ships calling from Sydney and Melbourne. The majority of transport of goods and passengers to and from the Shoalhaven continued from the Greenwell Point wharf until the extension of the railway reached Bomaderry in 1893.

By 1880, commercial fishing was well established, with much of the catch being shipped to the Sydney market. Oyster growing developed in the 1880's and is now a multi million dollar industry.

Greenwell Point's population now numbers approximately 1200, many of whom are involved in the commercial fishing, oyster growing or tourism industries. Many visitors to the town are attracted by its reputation for excellent fishing in the river, which yields catches of flathead, bream and mullet, while others come to sample the fresh oysters and famous fish and chips available on the waterfront.

Pyree

Originally part of the Berry Estate known as Upper Numbaa, Pyree is located between Nowra and Greenwell Point. The name is an aboriginal word meaning box trees, a reference to the timber which was once prolific in the area. Early European settlers - tenants of Alexander Berry who later bought their leases - cleared the land for farming, exporting their produce from Greenwell Point to the Sydney market. The area is now largely used for dairy farming.

The original school at Pyree, built from slab and shingle in 1860, was replaced in 1877 by a brick building which now houses the Shoalhaven Family History Society's research centre.

Left: Pelicans are a feature of the Greenwell Point foreshore, where they are constantly on the lookout for a feed from anglers cleaning their catch.
Below: Low tide at Greenwell Point reveals the extent of the oyster leases.

Culburra Beach and Orient Point

Best known as holiday destinations, these towns are famous for their beaches and their access to excellent ocean, river and rock fishing sites. Game fishing charters from Orient Point take anglers to the famous fishing grounds of `The Banks´ and the continental shelf, where marlin, kingfish and tuna are the prize catches.

Each summer the population of the both towns swells as tourists arrive to enjoy the sun, sand and surf, while warm evenings and weekends see Nowra residents flock to the surf beach at Culburra.

Culburra was originally known as Wheelers Point after the first European landholder George Wheeler, but the name was changed by developer Henry Halloran who purchased and subdivided the land. Walter Burley Griffin designed the subdivision which features the curved streets that were characteristic of his style.

Left: The towns of Orient Point and Culburra are completely surrounded by water. Orient Point (in the foreground), is bounded by the Crookhaven River and Curleys Bay, while Culburra is bounded by Lake Wollumboola to the south, Curleys Bay to the west and Culburra and Warrain Beaches to the east. Below: Sunrise at Culburra Beach.

Currarong

Currarong is located on the Beecroft Peninsula, northern headland of Jervis Bay, 33 kilometres south east of Nowra. Currarong Creek bisects the town's residential area, which consists of a mixture of holiday homes and permanent dwellings.

The area was little known until 1928 when the *SS Merimbula* ran aground on Whale Point, approximately 1.5 kilometres northeast of the present town. No lives were lost but many sightseers from around the district came to see the shipwreck, which had its bow wedged firmly on the rock shelf. The wreck has been a drawcard for visitors ever since, though very little of the bow section remains today.

The first permanent European settlers in the town were the Lamond Family, who arrived in 1932 and in 1936 the town's post office and telephone exchange opened. These days the town has a permanent population of 550, which swells to many times that number in the summer months when visitors flock to Currarong to take advantage of its proximity to Jervis Bay and the beach.

A small group of professional fishermen live in the town, and recreational anglers are also attracted by the excellent fishing. Land-based game-fishing on Beecroft Peninsula yields catches of yellowfin and kingfish, while salmon, flathead and bream are regularly caught on the beach. Just 12 kilometres off-shore 'The Banks' offers excellent game-fishing opportunities with marlin, kingfish and tuna regularly being hooked.

Much of the Beecroft Peninsula is protected within Jervis Bay National Park, which is immediately adjacent to the town. Several walking trails start at Abrahams Bosom Beach, the town's protected swimming beach. A short walk leads to the SS Merimbula Wreck and delightful Honeysuckle Point, while a longer walk to Mermaids Inlet leads to the rock platforms of Beecroft.

Point Perpendicular Lighthouse, Honeymoon Bay and Long Beach can be reached by a short drive from Currarong. The lighthouse and its adjacent cottages are classified by the National Trust. It is dramatically situated atop the vertical cliffs of Point Perpendicular, where rock-climbers are frequently seen tackling the challenging rock face.

Left: The Rock Pool is a natural swimming pool on the foreshore at Currarong
Above right: There are many popular rock climbing destinations throughout the Shoalhaven, but none as spectacular as Point Perpendicular.
Right: Drum and Drumsticks, an offshore island group adjacent to the Beecroft Peninsula, is a popular scuba diving destination.

Callala Bay and Callala Beach

These delightful towns on the northern side of Jervis Bay are separated by Callala Creek. The calm waters of the Jervis Bay are excellent for a variety of water based activities, including sailing, windsurfing, swimming and snorkelling. The Jervis Bay Cruising Yacht Club is based at Callala Bay, where many yachts are permanently moored.

While equally popular with residents and holiday makers, the growing population of permanent residents (now numbering more than 2,300) led to the opening of the Callala Beach Community Hall in 1996, the Callala Bay Community Centre in 1997 and Callala Bay School in 2000.

Myola

A small township on the shores of Currambene Creek, Myola is an aboriginal word meaning place of crabs. Myola boasts excellent flathead fishing in the creek.

Left: Callala Beach is a long expanse of white sand backed by low dunes. Dolphins are regularly seen close to shore.

Below: Callala Bay underwent a major upgrade of its foreshore facilities in 2000, including the construction of a jetty, reconstruction of the boat ramp, sealing of the car-park and construction of a building for the sailing school which provides storage facilities for junior sailing craft.

Huskisson

Situated where Currambene Creek enters Jervis Bay, Huskisson has always been a town with a strong association with the sea. In 1861 George Dent started building boats at the mouth of Currambene Creek and ship building soon became the town's major industry. One ship built by Dent was the Sydney Harbour ferry, the Lady Denman which was returned to Huskisson after decommissioning in 1979 to become the focal point of the Lady Denman Heritage Complex.

Also within the complex is the famous Bidjigal Aboriginal Arts and Crafts Centre and an exhibition gallery which will house travelling exhibits from other museums, stage art exhibitions and host concerts and special events. A major drawcard to the Lady Denman site is 'The Pond' which is filled with fish from Jervis Bay, many of which have grown very large thanks to the visitors who enjoy feeding them. Fishing is not allowed; the pond and its inhabitants are now protected within Jervis Bay Marine Park.

The major industry in Huskisson today is tourism, with several operators catering for the scuba divers who wish to experience the diverse marine life and exceptionally clear waters of the bay. Eco-tourism is a vital part of the industry with several boats offering visitors the opportunity to spot dolphins, whales, seals and penguins in their natural habitat. Humpback whales travel along the coast on their annual migration between June and November and southern right whales occasionally stay briefly in the bay. During the winter months Australian and New Zealand fur seals can be observed on the Bhewerre Peninsula and Bowen Island is home to a colony of little penguins which are often seen swimming and fishing in the bay.

Left: An aerial view of Huskisson showing Currambene Creek entering Jervis Bay. The mangrove ecosystem of the creek is an important fish nursery and also plays an important role in stabilising sediments and silt. A boardwalk with explanatory signs passes through the mangroves, starting at the Lady Denman complex.

Above Right: Dolphin, whale, seal and penguin watching tours depart daily from Huskisson. The bay is home to several pods of bottlenose dolphins; penguins nest on Bowen Island; seals winter on Bhewerre Peninsula and whales are spotted between June and November.

Right: The Lady Denman was built in Huskisson by George Dent in 1911 and served as a Sydney Harbour ferry from 1912 until 1979. Thirty four metres in length and weighing in at 96 tonnes, the Lady Denman was originally fitted with steam engines, which were replaced by diesel motors in 1936. In 1981 she was returned to Huskisson to become the centrepiece of the Lady Denman Heritage Complex. Over the years the Lady Denman has undergone massive restoration work to restore her to her former glory.

Vincentia

Originally known as South Huskisson, Vincentia was the first of the two towns to be settled, though by 1853 it had virtually been abandoned. When the developer Henry Halloran bought the land in 1951 only three houses remained but since then Vincentia has grown into a thriving bayside township with a permanent population exceeding 2,500.

Vincentia is a town of beautiful beaches; Collingwood Beach sweeps from Moona Moona Creek at Huskisson to the Vincentia boat ramp, east of which are Orion Beach and Barfleur Beach, home to the Vincentia Sailing Club. Around Plantation Point is Nelsons Beach, the tiny and isolated Nudist Beach, Blenheim Beach and Greenfields Beach, which is situated within the Jervis Bay National Park.

The land on Plantation Point rises steeply from the water, affording excellent views of Jervis Bay.

Left: An aerial view of Vincentia showing the sweeping Collingwood Beach and Plantation Point. Vincentia golf course can be clearly seen.
Below: Point Perpendicular and Bowen Island from Nelsons Beach. All Vincentia's beaches offer spectacular views across Jervis Bay to the heads.

Hyams Beach

Located on the shores of Jervis Bay a few kilometres south of Vincentia, Hyams Beach is famous for having the whitest sand in the world.

The beach affords a beautiful view south to the naval college HMAS Creswell and east across Jervis Bay to Point Perpendicular.

Dolphins are regularly spotted close to shore and sand whiting can be seen in the shallows. The area near the boat ramp is a safe and popular spot for shore-diving, where cuttlefish, Port Jackson Sharks and weedy sea dragons are regularly seen.

The general store at Hyams Beach has become a mecca for lovers of fine food and offers gourmet breakfasts, light meals throughout the day and an exciting restaurant menu in the evenings.

With a permanent population of little more than one hundred people, Hyams Beach is largely a holiday town, and offers a range of self-contained accommodation.

Left: Hyams Beach is famous for having the whitest sand in the world, a phial of which is displayed in the British Museum in London.
Below: An aerial view of Hyams Beach showing St Georges Basin in the background and Pigeon House Mountain on the horizon.
Above right: Sailing is a popular sport on Jervis Bay.

The Towns of St Georges Basin

Sanctuary Point, Basin View, St Georges Basin and Erowal Bay are townships fringing the northern shores of St Georges Basin while on the southern side, Sussex Inlet lies on a stretch of river joining St Georges Basin with the sea.

The first European settler in the region was Jacob Ellmoos, a Danish migrant who established a farm on the northern side of the river in 1880. His family were commercial fishermen but they soon became famous for their guest house, Christian's Minde, which opened in 1896.

The protected waters of St Georges Basin lend themselves to fishing, sailing, swimming and water skiing and the numerous boat ramps in the area give easy access to The Basin and the ocean.

The idyllic setting of The Basin has made the surrounding townships the fastest growing localities in the Shoalhaven region in recent years.

Left: Sunset at St Georges Basin.

Below: The jetty at Home Bay is an ideal fishing spot.

Swanhaven, Cudmirrah and Berrara

Swanhaven is a small township on the north-eastern shore of Swan Lake, immediately south of Sussex Inlet. Cudmirrah is sited on the southern shores of the lake and also fronts Cudmirrah Beach while Berrara is bounded by Berrara Creek and the beach.

Surrounded by water as all these towns are, it is not difficult to imagine that water sports are a major drawcard. Canoeing, fishing, sailboarding and water-skiing are popular on the sheltered waters of Swan Lake, while surfing, body-boarding and beach fishing are enjoyed from Cudmirrah Beach.

The total permanent population of the three towns is a little over 600, but the influx of tourists in the summer months sees the population increase many fold.

Left: The sheltered, calm waters of Swan Lake are ideal for a variety of water-based recreation activities including water skiing, sailboarding, canoeing and fishing.

Below: An aerial view of Berrara showing its delightful waterfront location, with its proximity to both the beach and Berrara Creek.

Bendalong, Manyana and Cunjurong Point

Located on the coast approximately half way between Sussex Inlet and Ulladulla, these three towns boast spectacular coastal scenery, and are a mecca for surfers and beach anglers.

At Bendalong, Boat Harbour Beach has a resident population of tame stingrays, who come into the shallows each day to be fed. Red Head separates protected Washerwoman Beach and Boat Harbour Beach (on the northern side of the headland) from Inyadda surf beach, which is reputed to have some of the finest breaks on the south coast.

Immediately south of Bendalong, Manyana and Cunjurong Point hug the coastline between Inyadda Point and Green Island, which can be accessed at low tide.

The towns of Conjola Lake

Conjola Lake is a magnificent expanse of water nestled between the Princes Highway and Conjola Beach. The lakeside towns of Fishermans Paradise, Lake Conjola West, Killarney and Lake Conjola all take advantage of the excellent fishing and water sports on the lake.

Left: An aerial view of Red Head and Bendalong showing Manyana, Cunjurong Point and Green Island in the distance.

Below: Inyadda beach offers some of the best surfing on the south coast.

Milton

Reverend Thomas Kendall was the first European to settle in the south of the region after taking up a grant of land near the present township of Milton in 1828.

Timber was the principal industry of the early days, when both cedar and hardwoods were cut and milled locally before being transported to Sydney, but these days much of the district is given over to dairy farming.

Milton's contemporary appeal owes much to its past; the many beautifully preserved historic buildings lend character and charm to this delightful town. The Settlers Fair on the October long weekend celebrates the early history of the town.

Mollymook

Located on the eastern side of the Princes Highway between Milton and Ulladulla is the township of Mollymook, famous for its excellent surfing beaches and the Hilltop championship golf course. The earliest settlers in the area were Henry and Ellen Mitchell who called their farm Molly Moke, probably after the Mollymawk, a specie of Albatross which visited the coastline in spring.

While Mollymook has been a popular leisure centre with locals since the early years of this century it is only in the last two decades that the town has grown into the leading tourist resort that it is today.

Ulladulla

Originally known as Boat Harbour, then as Wasp Harbour, Ulladulla was important in the early days of European settlement as the port for the township of Milton and the surrounding farming districts. It wasn't until well into this century that the Ulladulla population exceeded that of Milton and it became the centre of commerce in the south of the region. Today, the combined population in the Milton, Ulladulla area is approaching 12,000.

Professional fishing was started in the 1930's by three Italian families and today Ulladulla is home to the region's largest commercial fishing fleet. The annual `Blessing of the Fleet´ festival on Easter Sunday is a colourful spectacle which follows this Italian custom.

Burrill Lake

Just a few kilometres south of Ulladulla, Burrill Lake was named in 1828 by surveyor Thomas Florance. Like many of the towns in the south of the region it was originally a timber town, but these days tourism is the major industry.

Left: An aerial view of Ulladulla, showing its protected harbour, home to the town's commercial fishing fleet. Pigeon House Mountain can be clearly seen on the horizon.

The towns of the south

The Shoalhaven region extends approximately fifty kilometres south of Ulladulla and takes in the towns of Tabourie Lake, Bawley Point, Kioloa and Durras North, on the shores of Durras Lake.

The first European to settle in the area was Sydney Stephen. The manager's residence on his selection, built by convict labour, was called Murramarang House, and is still occupied today. In the early years of European settlement many of the southern Shoalhaven towns were timber towns and at one time the mill at Kioloa was reputed to be the largest in the southern hemisphere, employing more than 70 men.

Large tracts of the coastline south of Kioloa are now protected within Murramarang National Park, which is famous for its resident population of eastern grey kangaroos, who regularly take to the water for a cooling swim on hot summer days.

Campers started visiting the area in the 1920's to enjoy the beautiful, unspoilt beaches and excellent fishing, a past-time that remains popular to this day.

Left: Ten kilometres south of Ulladulla on the Princes Highway, Tabourie Lake is a poplar tourist destination. Crampton Island offers excellent fishing.

Below: Eastern grey kangaroos are regularly seen feeding on the grassed dunes adjacent to the beaches in the far south of the region.

PARKS

Within its total area of 466,250 hectares the Shoalhaven region has more than 300,000 hectares of parks, state forests and reserves. Seven Mile Beach, Booderee, Jervis Bay, Murramarang, Morton and Budawang National Parks, along with Jervis Bay Marine Park preserve a variety of important ecosystems while many smaller nature reserves exist throughout the region to protect specific plant and animal habitats. These parks and reserves also offer an enormous variety of recreational activities including fishing, surfing, bushwalking, rock climbing, birdwatching, scuba diving and canoeing.

THE PARKS OF JERVIS BAY

Over the years the pristine beauty of Jervis Bay has been threatened on many occasions. A steel mill was proposed for Currambene Creek in 1969, a nuclear power station was mooted for Murrays Beach in the 1970's and more recently, it was recommended that the East Coast Armaments Complex be relocated to Cabbage Tree Point on the Beecroft Peninsula. None of these development plans have come to fruition and Jervis Bay remains a place of outstanding natural beauty. Large sections of Jervis Bay are now protected in parks and reserves.

Booderee National Park

At the southern end of Jervis Bay, much of the land annexed from NSW in 1911 to provide a port for the national capital is now protected within the Booderee National Park. Included in this park are large sections of the Bherwerre Peninsula, Bowen Island and the southern waters of Jervis Bay.

Lying on the overlap of temperate and southern climatic zones, Booderee contains an astonishing number of plant and animal species. A wide variety of habitats has added to this diversity; dune systems, beaches, coastal cliffs, heaths, forests and swamps are all present within the park.

Within these diverse habitats a range of recreational activities are enjoyed by visitors to the park; Bherwerre, Cave and Steamers beaches offer excellent surfing; Green Patch offers delightful bush camping on the shores of Jervis Bay and there are a range of bush-walking trails from which to choose.

Aboriginal people have lived in the Jervis Bay area for more than 20,000 years and the park protects sites containing archaeological evidence of their traditional lifestyle. Booderee is jointly managed by the Wreck Bay Aboriginal Community and Parks Australia.

Left: The astonishingly clear waters of Jervis Bay have been protected within Jervis Bay Marine Park since 1998.

Booderee Botanic Garden

Located within Booderee National Park, the Botanic Garden covers an area of 80 hectares. The gardens have an emphasis on the flora of the coastal regions of southeast Australia and contain both natural and cultivated areas. Pleasant walks criss-cross the gardens and pass through natural bushland of scribbly gums and heath to the lush greenery of Rainforest Gully.

Jervis Bay Marine Park

Although the exceptional features of Jervis Bay's marine environment were recognised as worthy of protection as long ago as 1975, it wasn't until January 1998 that the Jervis Bay Marine Park was finally gazetted. Located at a mixing point of warm northern waters, cooler temperate waters and cold southern waters, Jervis Bay supports an enormous diversity of marine species including more than 200 species of fish and 200 species of invertebrates. A wide variety of habitats adds to this diversity and includes mangrove areas, intertidal zones, subtidal rocky reefs, caves, drop-offs, a variety of soft-bottom habitats and the most extensive sea-grass meadows in NSW. With no major rivers draining into the bay, its exceptionally clear water means that some species are found at much greater depths in the bay than elsewhere.

The long beaches of white sand, crystal clear water and prolific marine life attracts scuba divers, snorkellers, anglers, swimmers, surfers and sightseers to the Jervis Bay Marine Park. The bay also hosts visiting whales on their annual migration and boasts several pods of semi-resident dolphins. Dolphin, whale, penguin and seal watching trips are some of the new ecotourism-based activities which are becoming increasingly popular.

The Jervis Bay Marine Park aims to protect the exceptional marine heritage of the bay, whilst still allowing recreational and commercial activities to continue. To this end, particularly vulnerable areas such as sea grass meadows have been identified and are protected within sanctuary zones, while less sensitive areas will be managed on the principles of ecological sustainability.

Left: The tawny frogmouth (Podargus strigoides) is frequently heard, but not so commonly seen in the area.
Right: Humpback whales are frequently seen along the Shoalhaven coast between the months of June and November.

Seven Mile Beach National Park

Located on the coastline between Gerroa and Shoalhaven Heads, the 730 hectare Seven Mile Beach National Park preserves an important coastal dune system. The shifting foredunes are stabilised by hardy, salt-resistant spinifex while the permanently established dunes feature thickets of coastal tea-tree and wattle.

The park provides habitat protection for a variety of birds, including honeyeaters, thornbills and white-throated tree creepers. The long expanse of Seven Mile Beach offers excellent fishing and surfing, while walking trails allow exploration of the forest area behind the dunes.

Murramarang National Park

Declared a National Park in 1973, Murramarang is the southernmost park in the Shoalhaven region and covers more than 1700 hectares of coastal land south of Kioloa. Wasp, Grasshopper, O'Hara and Dawsons Islands are also included in the park, sections of which extend beyond the southern border of the Shoalhaven.

The predominant plant community in the park is spotted gums with an understorey of ancient burrawang palms, while rainforest pockets occur in the sheltered gullies around Durras Mountain. Grey ironbark, blackbutt and bangalay also appear, particularly in the more open forests closer to the coast, while smaller trees and shrubs such as she-oaks, geebungs and coast rosemary are the dominant coastal plant communities.

The extensive forests of the park are home to many animals, including the eastern grey kangaroo, swamp wallaby and red-necked wallaby. Finches, honeyeaters and a variety of sea birds are frequently sighted, and the large numbers of tame crimson rosellas and king parrots in the park delight visitors with their antics.

Murramarang's biggest attraction is undoubtedly its resident population of eastern grey kangaroos, which are frequently seen on the vegetated dunes at Depot and Pebbly Beach. Accustomed to humans, these gentle animals can be observed at close quarters as they crop the grass on the dunes and have even been seen taking to the water on hot summer days.

Left: Seven Mile Beach National Park stretches from Gerroa to Shoalhaven Heads, protecting a coastal dune ecosystem.

Swimmers, surfers and anglers have many beaches and headlands to choose from within Murramarang, while walkers who climb Durras Mountain are rewarded by spectacular views of the coastline and adjacent ranges. Another favourite pastime for visitors is exploring the park's undisturbed coastline, with its sand and shingle beaches, rocky headlands and fossil-bearing rocks.

Morton National Park

By far the largest park in the Shoalhaven region, Morton National Park covers an area of 162,000 hectares of escarpment from Bundanoon in the north to Pigeon House Mountain in the south. Characterised by sandstone plateaus and deep ravines, the park is a thickly forested wilderness dissected by fast flowing streams.

A great variation in the landform within the park provides habitats for a range of animals including kangaroos, wallabies, snakes, lizards and a variety of birdlife. Numerous rare and some endangered species are found within Morton, such as brush-tailed rock wallabies, ground parrots and tiger quolls. Rare plant species include Pigeon House ash, Budawang ash and Ettrema mallee.

The northern section of Morton protects a long stretch of the Shoalhaven River, both upstream and downstream from Tallowa Dam. In the south of the park Pigeon House Mountain dominates the landscape and is a popular destination for rock climbers attracted by the steep cliffs of the escarpment. For bushwalkers, the three hour hike to the summit offers magnificent views to the coast and south into adjoining Budawang National Park.

Budawang National Park

Adjoining the southern end of Morton National Park, this 16,000 hectare wilderness is inaccessible by vehicle. The open forests of the western slopes are dominated by peppermint gum while silvertop ash grow on the ridges and steep hillsides. The park also contains some of the most southerly patches of subtropical rainforest. Experienced bushwalkers enjoy the challenging walks in Budawang National Park.

Right: Within Barren Grounds Nature Reserve, the spectacular rock formations at Drawing Room Rocks are so named because they have weathered into table and chair shapes. Perched on the edge of the escarpment at Woodhill Mountain, west of Berry, the Drawing Room affords panoramic views to Broughton Head, Kangaroo Valley and along the coast

ARTHUR BOYD'S BUNDANON

In March 1993, artists Arthur and Yvonne Boyd made an extraordinary gift to the people of Australia. With an estimated value of more than $12 million, their gift included the properties of Bundanon, Riversdale and Eearie Park, along with an enormous collection of artwork, photographs and letters, spanning four generations of the Boyd family. Located on the Shoalhaven River near Nowra, the combined Bundanon properties total more than 1,000 hectares and in 1993 a public company, the Bundanon Trust, was established by the Government to manage and develop this important natural and cultural heritage.

Arthur and Yvonne Boyd fell in love with the Shoalhaven when they visited the Bundanon property in 1971. At that time it was owned by Sydney art dealer Frank McDonald and his partners Sandra and Tony McGrath. The Boyds became interested in purchasing a property in the area, but they were in London in 1973 when Riversdale, the property adjoining Bundanon, was placed on the market. McDonald sent them photographs and the sale was completed by mail! Several years later the Boyds purchased Bundanon.

The historic Bundanon homestead was built in 1866 for Dr Kenneth McKenzie, a Scot who had come to Australia thirty years earlier. The colonial mansion was constructed from sandstone quarried nearby and extensive use was made of cedar cut from the property. Boyd's timber studio, purpose built in the 1970's, is separated from the house by a delightful cottage garden filled with sculptures by members of the Boyd family.

The Bundanon Trust's artist in residence program is accommodated a short walk from the homestead and is open to practitioners in all art forms from Australia and overseas. The Artist's Centre hosts residencies to approximately 60 artists per year: musicians, sculptors, painters, composers, writers, poets, photographers and other artists stay for four to six weeks, drawing inspiration from each other and the unique environment of Bundanon.

Arthur Boyd found enormous inspiration in the Shoalhaven landscape and its influence is seen in the large body of work produced over the last twenty five years of his life.

The Bundanon property is open to the public each Sunday when visitors are treated to tours through the house, studio and grounds.

Left: The historic Bundanon homestead, built in 1866 from sandstone and cedar taken from the property is listed on the register of the National Estate.

Above Right: The so-called 'single man's hut' at Bundanon was the home of an aboriginal stockman who never married, and lived there all his life.

Right: The artist in residence studios at Bundanon.

The Arthur and Yvonne Boyd Education Centre

Located at Riversdale, the Arthur and Yvonne Boyd Education Centre hosts residential arts education programs, concerts and other special events. The imposing Glen Murcutt designed building was financed by the Trust and a one million dollar donation by Fred Street. It has been described as a masterwork of late twentieth century architecture, and has won many awards.

Offering panoramic vistas of the Shoalhaven River, the centre can accommodate up to 36 visitors, who have the opportunity to learn from programs based on the natural and cultural heritage of Bundanon.

Left: The Arthur and Yvonne Boyd Education Centre at Riversdale. Designed by architect Glen Murcutt, the building was constructed in 1999.

Below: Visitors to The Bundanon Trust properties have the opportunity to view many original works by Arthur Boyd, this one shown in Boyd's Bundanon studio

THE ROYAL AUSTRALIAN NAVY

HMAS CRESWELL

The Royal Australian Navy has played an important role in the history of the Shoalhaven region, dating back to the establishment of an officers' training college in 1913. Parliament decided to locate the college at Jervis Bay as part of its plan to develop a federal port there. During the construction phase training was based at Osborne House Geelong, but moved to Jervis Bay on completion of the buildings in 1915.

Between the years of 1916 and 1930 the college produced graduates who formed the backbone of naval officers serving both ashore and afloat. The harsh economic climate of the depression saw a restriction in the number of cadet entrants and in 1930 the college was forced to move to the Flinders Naval Depot in Victoria. The site was then used as a resort until 1958, when the college returned to Jervis Bay and was commissioned as HMAS Creswell.

In the early days, cadet entrants were as young as 13 years of age and their four year course finished with their matriculation. These days, only professional naval training is conducted; all tertiary education is undertaken at the Australian Defence Force Academy in Canberra. Professional training at the college includes courses for qualified men and women joining the RAN, and is designed to impart the service skills and knowledge required of all officers. In addition, skills training for junior officers is conducted by the RAN Staff Training School, while the RAN School of Survivability and Ships' Safety is the lead school for training personnel in nuclear, biological, chemical defence and damage control throughout the navy.

The HMAS Creswell base has a delightful location, built atop low cliffs which overlook the waters of Jervis Bay to Point Perpendicular and Bowen Island. In recognition of its historic significance and its special value for present and future generations, the entire area of the naval college has been placed on the register of the Australian Heritage Commission.

Visitors will appreciate the many fine historic buildings as well as the tame wildlife, which includes a resident population of more than 100 kangaroos. The college is open to the public on weekends and public holidays.

HMAS ALBATROSS

Soon after the Second World War was declared in 1939, a decision was made to build an airfield at Nowra Hill and in May 1942 the Royal Australian Air Force occupied the base. They were soon followed by the US Army Air Corps and the Netherlands East Indies Air Force. When the British Admiralty directed some of its naval forces to the South West Pacific in 1944 it required shore based facilities for the Royal Navy and its Fleet Air Arm. The RAAF Base at Nowra was considered an ideal location because of its proximity to Jervis Bay, which was large enough to accommodate the entire British Fleet. The Royal Navy's Fleet Air Arm began operations at Nowra in October 1944 but in 1946 the base reverted to RAAF control.

In July 1947 the Commonwealth Defence Council approved the formation of a Fleet Air Arm, to be controlled and operated by the Royal Australian Navy, with shore facilities based at Nowra. HMAS Albatross was commissioned on 31st August 1948.

Since then the base has continued to grow, and recent redevelopment has seen many of the older facilities at the Naval Air Station replaced, resulting in increased efficiency of the airfield.

These days, Albatross is the largest employer in the Shoalhaven with more than 1000 service and 300 civilian personnel. Service members and their families total more than 3000, and their contribution to the economy of the region is enormous, providing an estimated $67 million input to the local economy.

The contribution made by HMAS Albatross to the local community is not merely an economic one: over the years, bush fire and flood relief assistance have been provided as well as searches and rescues of bushwalkers and fishermen.

During the Black Christmas of 2001/2002 extensive support was provided to the local community including water bombing and fire spotting activities by Squirrel and Sea King helicopters, supplying airfield services and providing meals and accommodation for firefighter, emergency personnel and evacuees from the Shoalhaven area.

THE MUSEUM OF FLIGHT

The Museum of Flight is Australia's largest aviation and regional museum. Situated alongside the historic - and active - military airfield at HMAS Albatross, (birthplace of the Royal Australian Navy's Fleet Air Arm), the museum was established in 1974 as the Australian Naval Aviation Museum.

The museum's comprehensive and interactive displays examine many aspects of Australia's aviation history, both military and civil, with particular emphasis on the Fleet Air Arm's unique heritage. The museum has more than thirty vintage aircraft on display as well as weaponry, models, photographs and military memorabilia.

Air Shows, which are held twice yearly, are a major attraction. They feature demonstration flights by vintage and military aircraft along with exhibitions of formation flying and low-level aerobatics. A parachute display by the `Red Berets´, members of the army's parachute training school, is a highlight of the Air Show. Visitors also have the opportunity to view inside operational aircraft such as Sea King and Sea Hawk helicopters.

Left: A Sea Hawk helicopter from 816 Squadron during training exercises at Beecroft Peninsula, Jervis Bay
Photo courtesy of Photographic Section, HMAS Albatross
Right: One of the vintage aircraft on display at the Museum of Flight. This 1940's Piper Cub, was flown solo from England to Australia in the 2001 London to Sydney Air Race

INDUSTRY

From the earliest days of settlement the principal industries of the Shoalhaven region were timber and dairying, and both industries remain important to the economy of the region today. An active manufacturing sector now complements these traditional industries, boosting the local economy by over $450 million annually and providing more than 3,500 jobs.

Now recognised as the most popular tourist destination in New South Wales outside Sydney, the region's thriving tourism industry provides more than 6,000 jobs (25% of the total workforce) and boosts the local economy by a further $500 million per year, making it the region's largest industry.

Dairy Industries

Alexander Berry took up a grant of 10,000 acres (4,047 hectares) on the Shoalhaven River in January 1822 and in August the same year the first draft of 93 cattle were driven into the region by Hamilton Hume. In the early years the Shoalhaven was used as a breeding ground for young stock but by 1850's dairying was established as the chief industry of the district.

Since 1989, the number of dairy farms in the region has reduced from 250 to approximately 50, but milk production has increased from 30 to 50 million litres per annum. Dairy deregulation has seen the number of farms decrease, but the size of individual farms increase. The Shoalhaven flood plain has a viable long-term future for dairying, so this sector will remain an important one in the Shoalhaven economy.

Dairy Farmers Co-operative is the largest employer in the dairying sector, producing whole milk, modified milks, cream and condensed milk at the Bolong Road plant. A major market for Dairy Farmers is condensed milk which is exported to Japan, as well as specialised dessert products for fast-food chains in Australia.

The other major user of milk products in the region is Unicorn Cheese. Located at South Nowra the company produces brie and camembert cheeses for the Australian market.

Maritime Industries

Commercial fishing in the Shoalhaven region is centred at Ulladulla and Greenwell Point, with some smaller boats operating from other locations. The fishing industry at Ulladulla was started by three Italian families in the 1930's and the first trawler started operating from Greenwell Point in 1945. These days, trawlers from both ports fish the ocean bed for table fish such as flathead, john dory, red fish, ocean

Left: Shoalhaven Paper (foreground), Australian Co-operative Foods and Shoalhaven Starches - three of the region's largest employers - are located on the Shoalhaven River at Bomaderry

perch and ling; live-baiters from Greenwell Point target kingfish, tuna and bonito while long liners from Ulladulla target yellowfin, big-eye and southern blue-fin tuna for the lucrative sashimi market. A proportion of fish is sold in the local market, but most is transported to the Sydney market, where it is used for the domestic and Japanese sashimi markets.

Oyster farming has been established in the Shoalhaven and Crookhaven Rivers for more than 100 years but it wasn't until the 1970's that the industry began to expand to the size it is today. There are now more than 30 farmers supplying Shoalhaven, Wollongong and Sydney markets with the famous Sydney Rock Oyster.

The Shoalhaven has a long traditional of boat-building, going back as far as 1861 when George Dent started building his first boats at Huskisson. These days, a range of marine vessels are produced in the Shoalhaven, using the services of surrounding industries to provide components including stainless steel and fibreglass. Sydney Yachts, Carbontech Spars (makers of masts), Kennedy Shipwrights and light hovercraft manufacturer, Nell Fabrication, have their manufacturing plants at South Nowra; Jarkan (yachts), Hobie Cat (recreational catamarans) and Cobia Boats (rubber and fibreglass surf rescue boats) are located at Huskisson on Jervis Bay; and Advanced Technology Watercraft, producers of the innovative Solar Sailor technology, are located in Ulladulla.

Forest Industries

The cedar forests of the Shoalhaven region attracted the first pioneers to the area and provided the mainstay of the local economy in the early years of permanent settlement. The Shoalhaven River provided an easy means of transporting the timber to Sydney and by January 1824, less than two years after taking up a grant of land in the region, Alexander Berry had more than 628,000 feet of cedar ready for shipment. Timber getters were quick to realise the importance of other trees and ironbark was soon being cut for use as railway sleepers and bridge decking, while turpentine was used for wharf pylons due to its natural resistance to marine borer.

Cedar is now rare, but these days forest reserves of more than 60,000 hectares yield native timbers such as spotted gum, blackbutt, iron bark, turpentine, scribbly gum, bloodwood, stringybark and bangalay, and are managed on a sustainable yield basis. The climate and soils of the region are largely unsuitable for plantation pine and only small pockets exist south of Ulladulla. The timber is milled locally and used in the Shoalhaven, Wollongong and Sydney. The forestry industry is estimated to provides around 250 jobs and contribute about $15 million annually to the regional economy.

Wine Making

Wine making began in the region in 1976 when Sid Mitchell planted the first vines at Jasper Valley but since then wine makers have started operation at The Silos, Cambewarra, Coolangatta, Bundewallah and a number of smaller estates.

Production includes chardonnay, verdelho, cabernet sauvignon and the traditional shiraz, but a French hybrid known as chambourcin, ideally suited to the rainfall in the region, is also widely planted. While most grapes are produced locally, the wine making is usually contracted to larger wineries in the Hunter Valley.

Defence Industries

Since the Australian Navy's Fleet Air Arm was established at HMAS Albatross in 1948, the defence industry has been of major importance to the local economy. It now contributes an estimated $67 million in wages and salaries in the region, and employs 1,260 military and 350 civilian personnel. With the outsourcing of many of the activities previously carried out by military personnel, opportunities are available to local business to contract to the defence department, and to be involved in the $150 million upgrade of the base which commenced in 1998.

The Albatross Aviation Technology Park, located next to HMAS Albatross west of Nowra, was developed in response to the Defence Department's plans to develop HMAS Albatross, and now houses companies including Kaman Aerospace International and CSC. In addition, many small local industries provide products and services to Defence.

Shoalhaven Starches

Located on the Shoalhaven River, Shoalhaven Starches is part of the Manildra Group. The permanent workforce of more than 200 is complemented by contract labour to produce starch, gluten, glucose, fructose and ethanol. The company is the largest manufacturer of wheat starch, glucose and ethanol in Australia. Glucose is supplied to brewers, jam makers, and confectionery and ice cream manufacturers. Seventy percent of the company's production of starch is used in paper manufacture, with the balance taken up for use in confectionery and baking.

A valuable by-product of starch manufacture is ethanol, which is used in the production of methylated spirits, inks, dyes, cosmetics and pharmaceuticals. Shoalhaven Starches is the Australian leader in ethanol production and produces fuel grade ethanol for use as a component of petrol.

Shoalhaven Paper Mill

Built in 1956 on its site on the river due to its suitable water supply, access to rail transport and reliable supply of labour, Shoalhaven Paper began recycling paper in 1966. It is now the largest manufacturer of fine recycled papers and specialty paper products in Australia. It draws its raw materials from all over the country, in particular the eastern seaboard, and markets its products Australia-wide. Today the mill employs around 280 people, with an annual wages bill of $20 million.

Left: Cambewarra Estate Winery, one of the region's award-winning wineries

Shoalhaven Campus

The Shoalhaven campus of the University of Wollongong and Illawarra Institute of Technology opened at West Nowra in June 2000. Situated on 67 hectares of bushland four kilometres south west of Nowra, the campus has sweeping panoramic views of the upper Shoalhaven catchment.

The Shoalhaven campus is a component of the South Coast Education Network which also includes access centres at Batemans Bay and Bega.

Courses on offer through the University include Bachelors of Arts (Community & Environment), Business Administration, Commerce, Engineering, Science (Physics) and Information & Communication Technology. The Illawarra Institute of Technology has courses in business, information technology, marketing, accounting and office skills, available either part time or full time.

Establishment of the joint campus followed more than ten years of planning by the University of Wollongong and Shoalhaven City Council, which led first to the establishment of a pilot campus at Graham Park, Berry in 1993. Two years later the University of Wollongong lodged a development application for the Shoalhaven campus at West Nowra. The Nowra Local Aboriginal Land Council and the local Aboriginal community generously lifted their land claim on the proposed site and construction commenced in 1998. Classes commenced in 2000.

Left: The Shoalhaven campus at twilight.

Below: The campus is located at West Nowra, just four kilometres from the town centre and overlooking the Shoalhaven River catchment.

LIGHTSTORM PHOTO GALLERY

The Lightstorm Photo-Gallery in Berry displays an exciting collection of photographic prints by landscape photographers Sue and Brian Kendrick. Photographed largely on Linhof Master Technika and Art Panorama large format cameras, the collection features images from the Shoalhaven and around Australia.

Many of the images featured in this book, plus others not shown, are available framed or unframed in a range of sizes. A selection of framing styles is available.

Some of the most striking images from the Lightstorm collection are available as signed and numbered Limited Edition Prints.

Albert Court, Albert Street, Berry NSW 2533
Gallery Ph: 02 4464 3165